The Healthy Slow Cooker Cookbook:

Over 55 Flavorous and Easy Slow Cooker Recipes for Busy People

Teresa Moore

Your Free Gift

I wanted to show my appreciation that you support my work so I've put together a free gift for you.

Big Diabetic Cookbook:

101 Diabetic Recipes for Living Well with Type 2 Diabetes

Just visit the link above to download it now.

I know you will love this gift.

Thanks!

Table of Contents:

Introduction

Bream, fried with vegetables in the Instant Pot

Bream in sour cream with garlic in a Instant Pot

Pangasius baked under the herbs and cheese in the Instant Pot

Carp with sour cream in an Instant Pot

Baked alstoglik with cheese in a Instant Pot

Large carver with zucchini in the Instant Pot

Fish in foil in an Instant Pot

Stewed pike perch with tomatoes in an Instant Pot

Pike perch in cheese batter in the Instant Pot

Heck a couple in an Instant Pot

Braised fish with vegetables in a Instant Pot

Cod with sour cream in a Instant Pot

Cod with sour cream in a Instant Pot

Carp baked in foil in Instant Pot

Flounder in the Instant Pot

Cod for a couple in an Instant Pot

Baked mackerel with lemon in an Instant Pot

Coho with oranges in the Instant Pot

Alaska pollack with lemon

Sprats in the Instant Pot

Stuffed peppers in an Instant Pot

Buckwheat with minced meat in an Instant Pot

Cake with minced meat in the Instant Pot

Chicken soup with meatballs in a Instant Pot

A soup of meatballs in a Instant Pot -

Rice casserole with minced meat and cheese in a Instant Pot

Rice casserole with chicken mince and vegetables in a Instant Pot

Cake with potatoes and meat in an Instant Pot

Tartar pie with meat in the Instant Pot

Hedgehogs in the Instant Pot

Kugelis with mushrooms in the Instant Pot

Soup with minced meat and vermicelli in an Instant Pot

Soup with minced meat and rice in a Instant Pot

Lasagna in the Instant Pot

Cabbage rolls in the Instant Pot

Potatoes with minced meat in an Instant Pot

Delicious cutlets in a multi-bar steamer in an Instant Pot

Couple cutlets in a Instant Pot

Macaroni "in a Fleet" in a Instant Pot

Tasty meatballs in sour cream sauce in a Instant Pot

Meatballs in the Instant Pot

Meat casserole with mashed potatoes

Buckwheat with minced meat

Khanum with meat and potatoes

Spaghetti bolognese

Casserole with minced meat and vegetables

Meat pie with meat

Potato casserole with meat balls

Lazy dumplings

Meatballs in tomato sauce

Introduction

This book provides great new flavors to try in your slow cooker. These simple and delicious recipes will have your favorite Asian dishes waiting for you right when you get home. With the press of a button, you can make authentic dishes that are healthier and tastier than their restaurant counterparts.

Bream, fried with vegetables in the Instant Pot

Ingredients:

- Carcass of bream - 1 kg
- Butter - 10 g
- Fresh potatoes - 5 pieces
- Onions - 3 pieces
- Flour - 4 tablespoons
- Pepper and salt

Preparation:

1. Carcass bream should be gutted and thoroughly cleaned.
2. Roll the spices and salt to your liking.
3. Strain in flour.
4. Pour half a cup of water into the bowl for the Instant Pot.
5. Add, chopped, onions and potatoes.
6. Cook for forty minutes in the "Baking" mode.
7. Your appetizing fried bream with potatoes is completely ready.

Bream in sour cream with garlic in a Instant Pot

Ingredients:
- Carcass bream -1 piece
- Sour cabbage - 20 g
- Fresh sour cream - 200 g
- Garlic - 2 pieces
- Lemon - 1 piece
- Salt and spices for fish

Preparation:
1. It is necessary to wash the bream, gut it and carefully clean it;
2. Salt and add the spices to taste;
3. Stuff the whole with sauerkraut;
4. Spread the carcass of bream in sour cream;
5. In the gills of the fish put on a slice of garlic, and on top of the carcass lay a lemon;
6. In the "Baking" mode in the Instant Pot, bake the fish for twenty minutes on both sides.
7. The best seasonings for bream are: hops-sanely, dill, bay leaf. For stuffing fish, you can use buckwheat porridge, which is mixed with a boiled egg, instead of sauerkraut.

Pangasius baked under the herbs and cheese in the Instant Pot

Ingredients:

- Pangasius fillet - 500 g
- Greenery - 100 g
- Onion - 1 piece
- Carrots - 1 piece
- Sour cream 150 g
- Sunflower oil - 1 tablespoon
- Pepper and salt

Preparation:

1. If the fillet is frozen, it is first defrosted. Then rinse thoroughly with running cold water. The fillet is dried with dry paper napkins;
2. Finely chopped onions with greens. Dill, green onion, parsley, celery or coriander are suitable for the dish;
3. On a large grater, gently rub the cheese, and then carrot;
4. A bowl of Instant Pot oil is smeared with vegetable oil, and then all the necessary ingredients are laid out in it. At the very bottom is a fish fillet Pangasius. From above it is sprinkled with pepper and salt to your taste. Then put onions, carrots on it. All this is abundantly sprinkled with greens and poured sour cream. For fish, a fifteen percent sour cream is suitable.
5. After forming the dish, he is put in an Instant Pot for thirty-five minutes in the "Bake" mode. It is sprinkled with cheese twenty minutes after baking starts.
6. Cooked fish neatly spread on a wide plate, sprinkled with herbs and cheese.

Carp with sour cream in an Instant Pot

Ingredients:

- Carcass - 500 g
- Fresh sour cream - 1 glass
- Garlic - 2 pieces
- Parsley dill
- Oil melted - 2 tablespoons
- Spices and salt

Preparation:

1. To wash the carcass and carefully cleanse the scales, this is done in the opposite way to its growth. Chop the abdomen of the fish and remove all the insides and black film, if it is inside. Then rinse the carcass thoroughly with water and dry with paper napkins;
2. Finely chop garlic and mix it with fresh sour cream;
3. Parsley with dill finely chop;
4. Set the brewing mode in the multivariate. Put the butter in the bowl and melt it. Then roll the crucians in flour and gently lay them on the bottom of the bowl;
5. Fry the carcasses on each side for fifteen minutes. It should turn out to be a pleasant golden crust;
6. Fish should be salt and pepper to taste. Then set the "Quenching" mode for two hours and add the cooked sauce.
7. Your aromatic crucian carp is ready for sour cream. Serve dishes with potatoes or vegetable salads.

Baked alstoglik with cheese in a Instant Pot

Ingredients:
- Carcass of carp - 1 kg
- Mayonnaise
- Pepper and salt
- Fresh cheese - 200 g
- Vegetable oil

Preparation:
1. Fish should be thoroughly cleaned, then gutted all the insides, rinse thoroughly under cool water.
2. Place the carrot fillet on a cutting board, cut into neat pieces of two centimeters.
3. Fold the pieces into a bowl, then add the pepper and salt to taste. Stir and add mayonnaise. Stir again more thoroughly.
4. Cover with the film, cover the mixture and put in the refrigerator for two hours.
5. Rub the cheese on the grater.
6. Turn on the Instant Pot in the "Baking" mode. Heat the bowl a little and put marinated silver carrot into it. Sprinkle them with mashed cheese on top. Cook thirty-five to forty-five minutes.
7. Served this delicious and interesting dish in a hot form. To it the garnish from boiled rice or mashed potatoes perfectly approaches. Baked silver carp served hot. To the fish, serve a side dish, for example, mashed potatoes or boiled rice.

Large carver with zucchini in the Instant Pot

Ingredients:
- Large carcass - 1 piece
- Lemon - 1 piece
- Tomatoes - 2 pieces
- Onion - 1 piece
- Squash - 2 pieces
- Bulgarian pepper - 1 piece
- Vegetable oil
- Salt and pepper

Preparation:
1. Fish carcass must be cleaned, well gutted, rinsed under cool water. Cut off the head, tail and all fins. Cut the fillet into medium sized pieces.
2. Put chopped fillets in a bowl. Wash the lemon, cut it with thin rings. Squeeze a little lemon juice. Add it and chopped slices to the carver. Thoroughly mix everything, leave the mixture to marinate.
3. Brush and cut finely. Pour vegetable oil into the bowl. Turn on the Instant Pot in the "Baking" mode. Fry the onions.
4. Cut the zucchini rings with one tomato. Send them to a fried onion. Stir the vegetables thoroughly.
5. Large carver in an Instant Pot5 Pick up the pickled fish from a bowl and roll each slice in spices and salt. Send carver to the cooking vegetables.
6. Bulgarian peppers with the remaining tomatoes cut into rings. For each piece of fish lay on a ring of tomato and bell pepper.
7. To cook a carver, we need to "Quench" for two hours.

Fish in foil in an Instant Pot

Ingredients:

- Fish fillets - 1-2 pieces
- Tomatoes - 2 pieces
- Onion - 1 piece
- Fresh cheese - 150 g
- Spices for fish
- Sour cream or mayonnaise
- Food foil

Preparation:

1. The fish must be cleaned and rinsed thoroughly.
2. Cut the tomatoes into rings, cheese with plates and onions in half rings;
3. We put the food foil into a rectangle, in accordance with the size of the fish.
4. Spread the fish neatly in the middle and sprinkle with spices, then cover the fillet with sour cream or mayonnaise.
5. It is necessary to lay out the vegetables. First onions, then tomatoes - they need to be greased with mayonnaise, and then cover with cheese plates.
6. Bend the edges of the foil. Carefully, to prevent cracks and no juice.
7. Gently fold the foil with the fish into the Instant Pot. Prepare a dish thirty-thirty-five minutes in the "Bake" mode. It is necessary that the cheese is melted and covered the fillet completely.
8. The dish is ready. Serve it hot in a wide dish with your favorite side dish.

Stewed pike perch with tomatoes in an Instant Pot

Ingredients:
- Fillet of pike perch - 1 piece
- Carrots - 1 piece
- Onion - 1 piece
- Tomatoes - 2 pieces
- Spices and salt
- Vegetable oil - 2 tablespoons

Preparation:
1. For pike perch we prepare a "pillow" of vegetables. For this, the onion is cut with rings, the carrots rub on the usual medium grater.
2. In a bowl Instant Pot, it is necessary to add vegetable oil and fry in it onions with carrots in the mode "Baking".
3. Fish should be cut into small pieces and put on a bow with a carrot. Top with sliced tomatoes.
4. Cook the pike perch in just thirty-five minutes in the "Quenching" mode.

Pike perch in cheese batter in the Instant Pot

Ingredients:

- Fillet of pike perch - 500 g
- Vegetable oil
- Spices and salt
- Cheese hard - 150 g
- Eggs chicken - 3 pieces
- Flour - 3 tablespoons

Preparation:

1. Fish fillet should be cut in portions. Salt and pepper to taste.
2. We need to cook the dessert. To do this, the eggs are beaten, and spices, flour, and cheese are added.
3. We pour the vegetable oil into the bowl and heat it in the "Bake" mode. Pieces of fish dip into the batter and then fry each side for about fifteen minutes.
4. To get a crisp, pike perch must be laid out on paper napkins. So, we get rid of the excess oil.
5. Your fragrant and crispy pike-perch in batter is ready.

Heck a couple in an Instant Pot

Ingredients:
- hake - 400 g
- olive oil - 7 ml
- salt
- ginger root - 20 g
- ground coriander - 0.5 teaspoon
- basil - 30 g
- white ground pepper - 0.4 teaspoon

Preparation:
1. Heck needs to be defrosted. For rapid defrosting, do this in water with salt. Brush the carcass and rinse thoroughly. Put the fish on the paper napkins to dry. Then cut the fish into steaks.
2. We leave a few branches of basil, and the rest is very shallow. Ginger root rubbed on a greater, then put in a bowl and pour olive oil. Add white pepper, basil and coriander. To stir thoroughly.
3. Hake should be rubbed with salt and a mixture of spices and butter. If the fish is prepared entirely, then you need to make incisions in the carcass and put the spices in them.
4. Pour into the bowl six hundred milliliters of water. Put the fish steaks in a special container and place it in the bowl. Cook in steaming mode for thirty minutes.
5. Cook the hake laid on a wide plate. Decorate the dish can be twigs of basil, slices of lemon and pepper.

Braised fish with vegetables in a Instant Pot

Ingredients:

- Fish carcass for your taste - 1-2 pieces
- Carrots - 2-3 pieces
- Onion - 2-3 pieces
- Bulgarian pepper - 1 piece
- Spices and salt
- Vegetable oil

Preparation:

1. The carcass of the fish should be thawed, well cleaned, gutted, and then cut off the tail with fins and rinse very carefully. Fillet is needed on medium sized pieces. Please salt.
2. Pour the vegetable oil in the bowl and lay the fish pieces on the bottom. Fry them in the "Baking" or "Frying" mode. Set the timer for forty minutes.
3. After roasting the fish must be poured into a bowl of water, and then cook for ten minutes.
4. While stew is preparing the vegetables. Slice the onions finely, then grate the carrots on a greater. Pepper Bulgarian must be cut into strips.
5. After ten minutes, put the vegetables in the bowl. Salt them and continue cooking until the time runs out.

Cod with sour cream in a Instant Pot

Ingredients:

- Fillets or carcass cod - 1 kg
- Carrots - a few pieces
- Onion - several pieces
- Spice
- Mayonnaise - 1 tablespoon
- Sour cream - 2 tablespoons

Preparation:

1. The carcass of fish must be well cleaned, gutted and thoroughly rinsed, cut off any excess. Cut the fillets into slices in portions. Their thickness should not exceed two centimeters.
2. Peel the carrots with onions. Carrots cut not thick rings, and onions - half rings. For original design use knives with a shaped blade.
3. Fish with vegetables should be folded into a bowl, add seasonings, salt to taste.
4. Mayonnaise and sour cream should be mixed, and then spread the mixture with fish. If the sour cream is too greasy, then it can be diluted with a small amount of water.
5. Turn on the Instant Pot in the "Quenching" mode. Prepare the dish for fifty to sixty minutes.
6. Your fish is ready. For a side dish, use boiled potatoes or rice with vegetables. You can try to cook cauliflower with fish, which will become an interesting side dish.

Cod with sour cream in a Instant Pot

Ingredients:

- Fillets or carcass cod - 1 kg
- Carrots - a few pieces
- Onion - several pieces
- Spice
- Mayonnaise - 1 tablespoon
- Sour cream - 2 tablespoons

Preparation:

1. The carcass of fish must be well cleaned, gutted and thoroughly rinsed, cut off any excess. Cut the fillets into slices in portions. Their thickness should not exceed two centimeters.
2. Peel the carrots with onions. Carrots cut not thick rings, and onions - half rings. For original design use knives with a shaped blade.
3. Fish with vegetables should be folded into a bowl, add seasonings, salt to taste.
4. Mayonnaise and sour cream should be mixed, and then spread the mixture with fish. If the sour cream is too greasy, then it can be diluted with a small amount of water.
5. Turn on the Instant Pot in the "Quenching" mode. Prepare the dish for fifty to sixty minutes.
6. Your fish is ready. For a side dish, use boiled potatoes or rice with vegetables. You can try to cook cauliflower with fish, which will become an interesting side dish.

Carp baked in foil in Instant Pot

Ingredients:

- Carcass or carp fillet - 1 piece
- Onion - 150 g
- Carrots - 150 g
- Fresh sour cream - 2 tablespoons
- Dill
- Garlic - 2 pieces
- Black pepper powder
- Salt
- Vegetable oil - 2 tablespoons

Preparation:

1. Carp need to be cleaned well.
2. The fish should be salted on all sides and leave for a few minutes.
3. It is necessary to prepare the filling. To do this, squeeze the garlic through a garlic squeezer. Cut the onions into half rings and grate the carrots.
4. It is necessary to warm up the bowl. To do this, set the "Baking" mode and hold for eight minutes. Then throw into the bowl onions, garlic, carrots and add vegetable oil. Fry until onion is transparent, regularly stirring.
5. It is necessary to chop dill and mix it with sour cream. Add the toasted vegetables to the resulting sauce. Stir thoroughly. Pepper and salt the filling.
6. We stuff the carp with stuffing. We spread out the food foil in several layers and spread the carp onto it.
7. We carefully pack the fish in foil and send it to the Instant Pot.
8. We cook for forty minutes in the "Bake" mode.

Flounder in the Instant Pot

Ingredients:

- Take 600 g of flounder
- Water - 0.5 cup
- 2 tablespoons sunflower oil
- 1 tablespoon of mayonnaise
- 1 piece of carrot
- 1 piece onion
- salt, spices

Preparation:

1. Before cooking, flounder should be gently cleaned, remove all existing insides, cut off the head. Be sure to remove all the bones. Remove the skin from the carcase to rid of its fishy smell. The fish should be thoroughly rinsed. Salt the fillets and cut them into chunks.
2. Peel the onions together with the carrots. Slice them into small pieces. Carrots can be rubbed through a greater.
3. Set in your Instant Pot mode "Baking" to fry on ordinary vegetable oil vegetables. Turn off the mode.
4. Pieces of flounder necessarily grease with mayonnaise, then send to the Instant Pot. Fill with water. Put the cook in the "Quenching" mode for about half an hour.
5. After the sound signal, take the cooked dish. Serve useful, very tasty, fragrant fish only in a hot form with a garnish of mashed potatoes.

Cod for a couple in an Instant Pot

Ingredients:
- 450-500 g cod fillets
- Cold water - 500 ml
- fish seasoning and salt

Preparation:
1. It is necessary to thoroughly wash the cod fillets under cool water. Cut it into several serving slices.
2. Well chop each piece with salt and fish seasoning. Accurately with the salt, because in the seasoning it already exists. Leave the fish fillets for about fifteen minutes.
3. Pour cold water into the bowl for the Instant Pot, then in it you need to lower a special basket for steaming. It is necessary to carefully put in it the pickled pieces of cod. Set the mode for the Instant Pot "Boiling on water steam" for just twenty-five minutes.
4. Already ready, aromatic fish to serve hot. As a side dish, stewed vegetables are perfect.

Baked mackerel with lemon in an Instant Pot

Ingredients:
- Mackerel without head - 1.5 kg
- 2 small lemons
- fish spices, salt and pepper

Preparation:
1. Cut off all fins from fish fins and rinse them thoroughly. Cut them into two, three equal parts. Make on the fillets uniform cuts, so that you can place slices of lemon;
2. Mackerel must be salted, peppered and sprinkled with spices so that nothing gets into the incisions;
3. Put lemon slices into the incisions on the fish pieces;
4. In a bowl for Instant Pot put mackerel and pour fifty milliliters of cold water;
5. Set the multi-bar to bake and cook the fish for no more than thirty minutes;
6. Baked fish is ready. Aroma mackerel should be in hot form and decorate it with branches of fresh greens.

Coho with oranges in the Instant Pot

Ingredients:

- Fish fillet of coho salmon - 2 pieces
- Processed cheese - 200 g
- Orange - 1 piece
- Sunflower oil
- Lemon juice
- pepper, salt

Preparation:

1. Rinse each piece of coho smoothly with cool water. Dry them with paper napkins;
2. Lomti should be peppered, salt to your taste and sprinkled with lemon juice;
3. Orange wash and thinly cut into half rings. Fruit can be replaced with a tomato, for those who do not like this combination. The fish will have a different taste, but it will not make it less tasty and appetizing;
4. In advance, lubricate the bottom of the bowl for the Instant Pot with sunflower oil. Put in it the prepared fillet of coho salmon. On fish pieces lay the sliced orange, and on it slices of melted cheese;
5. Coho should be cooked for only twenty minutes with the "Hot" mode;
6. Finished fish is served hot and is decorated with fresh, sliced greens.

Alaska pollack with lemon

Ingredients:

- 2 carcasses pollock frozen
- 1 tablespoon lemon juice
- 2 teaspoons of fish seasoning

Preparation:

1. If pollock is frozen, then it must be thawed, well cleaned, remove fins, heads, entrails with black film. Cut the carcass into chunky pieces. Each of them must be cut a little diagonally. Rub lemon juice and fish seasoning. Leave to stand for one hour;
2. Along with the pollack, boil vegetables on the steam. For example, carrots and mushrooms. In addition to the Instant Pot bowl, add one glass, pre-washed, rice. Pour all the salted cold water;
3. The pollock should be cooked for ten to fifteen minutes, cook in steaming mode. Now your fish is ready.

Sprats in the Instant Pot

Ingredients:
- freshly frozen capelin - 1 kg
- black tea leaf - 1 tablespoon
- salt - ½ tablespoons
- granulated sugar - 1 tablespoon
- bay leaves - 5 pieces
- vegetable oil - 150 ml
- black pepper fragrant - 10 pieces
- water 150 ml

Preparation:
1. First, we need to clean the fish. For this, we defrost it, wash it in water, then we need to cut off the head, cut the abdomen and clean the black film, then rinse again.
2. We put the capelin into the cup of the Instant Pot so that it completely covers the bottom. Add to the fish the peppercorns and laurel leaves.
3. The next step is to make tea. If you brew loose tea, then please pour it through the strainer to avoid getting tea leaves into the dish. Tea should be brewed very strong, then add sugar and salt to it.
4. The resulting liquid is filled with capelin, and there we pour vegetable oil.
5. The contents of the Instant Pota under oppression, pre-covered with a plate.
6. In the menu, select the "Quenching" program and close the lid of the device for 40 minutes.
7. A couple of times during cooking, the fish should be checked, because water can boil out faster than you expect, and fish will burn.
8. After the sound signal, you can open the lid, remove the pressure, remove the laurel and pepper from the bowl.

Stuffed peppers in an Instant Pot

Ingredients:
- Bulgarian pepper - 4 pieces
- Minced beef - 500 g
- 150 grams of rice
- Water - 150 ml
- Spice

Preparation:
1. First you need to rinse and boil the rice.
2. While rice is being cooked, it is possible to prepare peppers for the stuffing: you need to wash the peppers and carefully remove the core and all the grains.
3. Welded rice mixed with minced meat. Add spices and salt to taste.
4. Now you can begin to stuff the peppers. For this purpose, it is best to use a small spoon (tea or dessert).
5. Using a spoon, shift the rice with minced meat into the pepper, pressing a little, "ramming" the filling with a spoon.
6. Put the peppers in the bowl of the Instant Pot.
7. Pour the peppers with water.
8. In the Instant Pot menu, select the "Quenching" program. Using the "Time of cooking" button, set the timer - 40 minutes.

Buckwheat with minced meat in an Instant Pot

Ingredients:

- Buckwheat groats - 2 cups
- Minced meat - 300 g
- Water - 3.5 cups
- Champignons - 350 g
- Bulb - 2 pieces
- Carrots - 1 piece
- Cooking salt
- Vegetable oil

Preparation:

1. Buckwheat first should be sorted, preferably several times. Remove black grains from it, then rinse it under the tap. Rinse with cold water.
2. Champignons too, rinse, then cut into slices. If they are frozen, do not defrost them.
3. Bulbs clean and chop thin half rings.
4. Carrots, too, clean and grate.
5. Wash meat, then pass through a meat grinder. Add salt and pepper to taste.
6. In a bowl Instant Pot pour a little vegetable oil, set the mode "Baking" for 20 minutes. Put the vegetables there and sauté, stirring occasionally.
7. After 10 minutes, put the vegetables to ground and continue frying in the same mode.
8. Then switch to "Buckwheat", or, if you do not have such a mode, "Kashu". Pour rinsed buckwheat and chopped mushrooms. Also, it is necessary to salt to taste. You can add your favorite spices and peppers.
9. Prepare our porridge will be for half an hour.

Cake with minced meat in the Instant Pot

Ingredients:

- Milk - 1 glass
- Sugar - 1 tablespoon
- Dry active yeast - 2 teaspoons
- Salt - 1 teaspoon
- Sunflower oil - 3 tablespoons
- Flour - 400 g
- Onion - 2 pieces
- Salt
- Minced meat - 450 g

Preparation:

1. To prepare the dough in warm milk, you need to dissolve the yeast with sugar and a few spoons of flour. The resulting mixture is set aside for half an hour, so that it begins to wander.
2. After the made mixture is formed frothy cap, it is added salt, sunflower oil and flour. Knead the dough.
3. We put the dough in a warm place, so that it rises and increases two times. For this it is very convenient to use an Instant Pot, in which you can set the temperature at 30 degrees.
4. While our dough rises, let's deal with the filling.
5. Onions are cleaned and finely shredded. There are two options for adding minced meat with onions to cake. You can put all raw, but you can pre-fry a little. If you decide to mince and fry onions, then be careful, and, spreading the filling in a pie, try not to get their meat juice.
6. Roll the dough into a thin layer. We lay out the stuffing on it and wrap the dough in a roll. Cut the resulting roll into equal parts with a height of approximately 7-10 cm.
7. We lubricate the bowl of the Instant Pot and spread out the small rolls on it. We turn on the "Heating" program for 15 minutes, and let the cake rise, about half an hour.
8. After this time, start the "Baking" mode, for one hour.
9. After the Instant Pot signaled the end of cooking, you need to turn the cake over to the other side and continue baking for another 20 minutes.
10. We take the prepared pie from the bowl, let it cool down a bit and serve it to the table.

Chicken soup with meatballs in a Instant Pot

Ingredients:
- Chicken mince - 250-300 g
- Potatoes - 300 g
- Onion - 1 piece
- Carrots - 1 piece
- Rice - ½ cup
- Water 2.5 liters
- Sunflower oil
- Semolina - 3 tablespoons
- Greenery
- Salt, pepper, spices

Preparation:
1. Chicken mince overwind in advance. It is good to salt, pepper and mix it. From the stuffing to form meatballs and tuck them in a manga.
2. Onion and carrots peel and wash. Then chop the onion and grate the carrots on a medium grater. Pour in a pan of Instant Pota sunflower oil and fry the chopped vegetables until soft. To do this, select the "Frying" mode. If this function is not available, then you can use the "Baking" mode. Roasting time 10 minutes.
3. Peel the potatoes from the peel and cut into cubes or brusochki. Then send the Instant Pot in a pan and pour water into it.
4. Rice carefully wash in water and add to the soup. Then send the ready-made meatballs.
5. Salt, pepper and throw spices that are suitable for soup.
6. Close the Instant Pot and select the "Soup" function. Most models are set automatically. If there is no such function, then the timer should be set for 45 minutes.
7. When the end-of-mode signal sounds, open the Instant Pot and add chopped dill or parsley. If there is umbrella dill, then they cannot be cut, and add whole. After they can be removed.
8. Close the lid and let the soup brew for 10 minutes on heating.
9. Now the soup is completely ready. It can be poured on plates and served to the table.

A soup of meatballs in a Instant Pot -

Ingredients:

- minced meat - 500 g
- potatoes - 3-4 pieces
- onion - 1 piece
- carrots - 1 piece
- rice - 3 tablespoons
- salt, pepper, spices
- chicken egg - 1 piece
- Bay leaf
- fresh greens
- water

Preparation:

1. We prepare meatballs. If frozen meat is used, it must be defrosted in the microwave beforehand or left for a few hours in a warm room.
2. In the dishes with minced meat, drive the egg, salt, pepper, add a little chopped onion. Very carefully we mix.
3. From the received weight we roll down meatballs of the desired size.
4. Preparing the vegetables. Potatoes are good for washing, we clean and cut into cubes. Carrots are cleaned and rubbed on a large grater. The bulb is cleaned, rinsed under running water, cut into half rings.
5. In a bowl Instant Pota spread the crushed potatoes, carrots, onions and harvested meatballs. Add spices to taste, salt, pepper, do not forget to put a bay leaf. Fill all with water.
6. Close the cover of the Instant Pot and set it to the "quenching" mode for 1 hour.
7. We rinse the rice with cold water and add to the bowl Instant Pota, when there are about 20 minutes before cooking. Mix and leave to cook until the Instant Pot beeps.

Rice casserole with minced meat and cheese in a Instant Pot

Ingredients:
- Minced meat - 0.5 kg
- Rice - 4 cups
- Onions - 1 piece
- Tomatoes - 800 g
- Cream - 300 ml
- Mozzarella - 130 g
- Garlic - 1 piece
- Basil, oregano, dried
- Allspice
- Salt

Preparation:
1. First, boil the rice. When it is ready, it can already be laid out in a bowl, which before it to oil a little oil, so that the casserole is not burnt. The first layer is ready.
2. Bulb clean and grind. Then stir with minced meat. Salt, you can pepper, add your favorite spices. From ground meat roll balls. Then put it over the rice in the bowl.
3. Now you can make a filling for the casserole. To do this, you need 2 cans of tomatoes in your own juice. Cut them into small pieces, lay out the third layer.
4. Mozzarella too finely chopped. Put it in the bowl, while it is ready, it will melt.
5. Garlic squeezed, mix it with cream and spices. Pour into the preform for the casserole.
6. It remains to include "Baking". It takes 40 minutes for this interesting dish to cook.

Rice casserole with chicken mince and vegetables in a Instant Pot

Ingredients:
- Chicken breast - 800 g
- Rice - 200 g
- Cream - 100 ml
- Carrots -1 piece
- Eggplant -1 piece
- Eggs - 2 pieces
- Bulgarian pepper - 1 piece
- Zucchini - 1 piece
- Parsley - bundle
- Garlic - 3 pieces
- Salt, condiments
- Sunflower oil - 30 ml

Preparation:
1. Rice to put cooked. Turn it off when it is half ready.
2. Meat grind in a meat grinder, then mix with egg, parsley, salt and spices. Mix. Then mix with minced meat and rice.
3. Next, we need a silicone culinary paper. She needs to install the capacity of the Instant Pot. Lay out the forcemeat and level it.
4. Squash, carrots, peppers and eggplant rinse, peel and chop. Carrots after that scald with boiling water. It is necessary for it to become softer and more plastic.
5. After that, vegetables should be added to minced meat, drowning them in it. To make it beautiful, colors should be alternated and laid out, having concentric circles.
6. Garlic finely chopped. You can use a garlic. Pour oil, pepper and salt to it. Stir. Then pour the egg and cream, then you need to use a mixer or fork to whip the mixture.
7. Pour the sauce over the casserole. Now it's left for 50 minutes to set the mode "Casserole".

Cake with potatoes and meat in an Instant Pot

Ingredients:

- Yeast dough - 1 kg
- Pork - 1 kg
- Potatoes - 600 g
- Onion (onion) - 200 g
- Oil (vegetable) - 1 tablespoon
- Salt, pepper, bay leaves

Preparation:

1. My meat, rubbed with a towel to remove excess moisture. Cut into small cubes.
2. Potatoes and onions are cleaned, cut into pieces of medium size: onion - half rings, potatoes - slices or slices.
3. Mix onion, meat and potatoes. Add salt, pepper, spices to taste and mashed laurel leaves. Once again, thoroughly mix, trying to avoid excessive discharge of liquid. If it does, it must be drained.
4. We completely lubricate the bowl of the Instant Pot oil from the inside.
5. We put 2/3 of the dough into the bowl, trying to level it and give it the shape of a container.
6. For the dough, put a mixture of potatoes, meat and onions, distributing evenly inside the Instant Pot.
7. The remaining third of the test is rolled out with a rolling pin, pierced with a fork in many places. This is done so that the dough does not rise when the hot air starts to rise while cooking.
8. Cover the filling with a batter. Fix the edges, connecting the bottom layer of the dough with the top.
9. Close the cover of the Instant Pot, open the steam valve. Turn on the "Baking" for 80 minutes. As soon as the Instant Pot is turned off - open the lid and leave the cake for a few minutes to cool down.

Tartar pie with meat in the Instant Pot

Ingredients:
- Dough (yeast) - 500 g
- Meat (pulp) - 500 g
- Onion (onion) - 2 pieces
- Egg (chicken) - 1 piece
- Kefir (sour cream) - 50 ml
- Potatoes - 300 g
- Broth - 100 ml
- Oil (vegetable) - 30 g
- Salt pepper

Preparation:
1. Meat washed, we remove water and chop into small pieces.
2. Onions and potatoes are mine and clean. Chop onion as small as possible. We cut potatoes with lobules or rings.
3. In a separate bowl, put onions, chopped meat, break the egg, add kefir. Kefir can be replaced with sour cream or curdled milk. Salt and peppers at will. It is worth remembering that meat absorbs a lot of salt, so it is better to add spices a little more.
4. All the contents of the bowl are carefully kneaded and left in a cool place for at least an hour, preferably two.
5. The finished dough is divided into two parts (1 to 3). The smaller part is rolled out with a thin layer, from the greater part of the test we make a dense "cover".
6. We spread the bowl of the Instant Pot oil on the bottom. We put a small part of the rolled dough into it.
7. On top of the dough, spread potatoes mixed with minced meat and cabbage.
8. On the filling carefully put the remaining dough, clamping the edges of both layers.
9. In the top layer of the dough, we pierce several holes with a knife or fork so that the steam leaves. One hole in the middle we do more. There we fill half the broth.
10. Close the Instant Pot and set the "Bake" mode for half an hour. As soon as the Instant Pot is turned off, open it and add the rest of the broth to the large hole in the test.

11. We close again and put the "Bake" for another half an hour. Once the Instant Pot is turned off, leave the cake to cool down a little.

Hedgehogs in the Instant Pot

Ingredients:

- minced meat - 0,5 kg
- rice - 0.75 cups
- water - 1 glass
- onions - 1 piece
- finely chopped cabbage - 3-4 tablespoons
- chicken egg - 1 piece
- salt - 1 teaspoon
- ground black pepper
- tomato sauce - 1 tablespoon
- low-fat sour cream - 2, 5 tablespoons
- greens, dried and fresh

Preparation:

1. To make hedgehogs in Instant Pot, first you need to prepare forcemeat. If we use frozen meat or meat for scrolling, we must give it a thaw beforehand. Boil the rice according to the traditional recipe, observing the proportion of rice and water 1: 2. Better to slightly not cook rice. It will reach the readiness in the process of preparing the hedgehogs themselves.
2. In the prepared forcemeat we put rice, finely chopped onions, crushed cabbage. Add salt and pepper to taste. Thoroughly knead to homogeneity. You cannot allow the formation of rice balls in minced meat.
3. In a separate deep bowl, mix tomato sauce with sour cream. Preparing the greens. If you use fresh, then you must thoroughly wash it and finely chop it.
4. From the prepared forcemeat we make small round hedgehogs. To avoid the difficulty of sticking the mass to your hands, you need to moisten your hands with plain water. We put the first batch on the bottom of the multivariate cup, pre-lubricated with butter.
5. Each meat ball needs to be coated with tomato-sour cream sauce and sprinkled with greens on top.
6. We make the next batch of hedgehogs from the second stuffing. Put the second layer in the multivariate cup. Also, spread the sauce and sprinkle with herbs.
7. In the remainder of the sauce, add a little water, mix and pour the hedgehogs. Sauce should not cover them completely. It is necessary that he reach only the middle of the first layer.

8. Now it's time to load the cup into the Instant Pot and set the required parameters. It is necessary to carefully extinguish them for 1 hour and 15 minutes.

Kugelis with mushrooms in the Instant Pot

Ingredients:
- 800 g minced meat
- 1 kg of potatoes
- 2 pieces of onions
- 3 tablespoons flour
- 2 eggs
- 2 tablespoons vegetable oil
- 200 g of mushrooms
- salt and pepper

Preparation:
1. We begin with the onion. That is, it should be lightly fried in a frying pan. At the same time, it should be crumbled very finely, and it is necessary to fry with mushrooms.
2. When mushrooms and onions are fried, add the prepared stuffing there. It should be fried until ready.
3. Then proceed to the potatoes. Naturally, it must be cleaned, washed and rubbed on a fine grater. By the way, it is not important to rub, it is possible and, in a blender, to make mashed potatoes from raw potatoes, and to twist in a meat grinder with a small sieve.
4. In the mashed potatoes, which is obtained after the above procedure, you need to drive in the egg and add flour. It is necessary for giving viscosity to the mass.
5. Let's go to the Instant Pot. The bowl should be oiled with vegetable oil and sprinkle a little with flour.
6. Potato mass, which was cooked in advance, is divided into two equal parts. The first part is laid out on the bottom of the bowl. The second layer is laid fried with onions and mushrooms forcemeat. The third is the second part of the potato mass.
7. Next you need to look at what a Instant Pot company is. The main difference between Redmond and Panasonic. In the first case, the cooking takes place in two stages. First 60 minutes in the "Soup" mode, and then 10 minutes in the "Rice" mode. In the second case, the "Baking" mode with automatic time is simply turned on.

Soup with minced meat and vermicelli in an Instant Pot

Ingredients:

- Minced meat - 400 g
- Potatoes - 4 pieces
- Vermicelli
- Carrots - 1 piece
- Onion - 2 pieces
- Egg - 1 piece
- Bay leaf
- Salt, spices, herbs
- Vegetable oil

Preparation:

1. Clean and rinse onions with carrots. We shared a bulb finely, carrot three on a greater.
2. We pour a little vegetable oil into the bowl of the Instant Pota. Turn on the "Frying" mode, if there is no such program, then "Baking" will do. For about ten minutes on the hot oil, fry the crushed carrots and onions.
3. We clean potatoes with small cubes. Several times it is washed, that would get rid of excess starch. Thanks to this trick, when boiling up the soup, very little potato foam will form.
4. Add the crushed potatoes to the fried vegetables. Fill all the necessary amount of broth or water. If cooking soup on the water, then salt, put the bay leaf and spices to your taste.
5. Now let's cook meatballs. In the stuffing you need to put salt and pepper to taste, raw egg and very finely chopped onions. You can grind the minced meat with onions in a meat grinder. This will allow you to mix meat and onions more thoroughly. All very carefully mix and form small balls. To make it easier to mold them out of minced meat, hands should be periodically moistened with water. You can immediately make meatballs and put them in soup.
6. Now the Instant Pot can be transferred to the program "Quenching" or "Soup". The cooking time also depends on how you cook. If the soup is brewed on ready-made broth, then enough for 30-40 minutes. If you cook on the water, the time will take a little more than an hour.
7. Minutes for 15 before the end of cooking in the dish you need to add vermicelli. Try to mix the soup several times to avoid sticking the vermicelli

to the bottom of the Instant Pot bowl. Unfortunately, with all the wonderfulness of the bowl, vermicelli, when lumped, sinks to the bottom and sticks there, so stirring soup will be an important point.

8. Then you need to add fresh and chopped dill, parsley, green onions.
9. Soup with meatballs and vermicelli is ready.

Soup with minced meat and rice in a Instant Pot

Ingredients:
- Minced meat - 350 g
- Potatoes - 3 pieces
- Carrots - 1 piece
- Onions - 1 piece
- Bulgarian pepper - 1 piece
- Tomato - 1 piece
- Rice - 1 measuring cup
- Salt, spices, herbs
- Vegetable oil

Preparation:
1. Bulb and carrots mine, clean and finely shred. Carrots can be cut or grated.
2. We turn on the Instant Pot, the program "Frying" or "Baking". In the bowl pour a little vegetable oil and fry the chopped onions and carrots.
3. Then in the bowl you need to add peeled and chopped Bulgarian pepper and minced meat. It is not necessary to overcook very much, enough for 5 to 7 minutes, no more. After that, add tomato paste or crushed tomatoes to the frying pan. Then pour a small amount of water or broth, literally, a couple of ladles, and let's extinguish a few more minutes.
4. Finely chop the potatoes, rinse it. Also, very carefully washed rice, at least 5-7 times. This will avoid the formation of a strong foam when cooking. Add the potatoes and rice to the bowl of the Instant Pot.
5. Fill it all with the necessary amount of water or broth.
6. Soup with minced meat in a multivariate
7. If you cook on the water, then salt, put the laurel leaf and your favorite spices.
8. Switch to the "Soup" or "Quenching" mode for approximately one hour.
9. In the end, add fresh greens.

Lasagna in the Instant Pot

Ingredients:

- 400 g of premium flour
- 4 eggs
- 4 tablespoons olive oil
- A little salt
- 600 g minced meat from pork and beef
- Large onion
- 1 carrot
- 100 g of tomato paste
- Sweet red pepper
- Parsley
- Salt, pepper, dried basil, oregano, rosemary
- 250 ml of creamy cream
- 250 grams of hard cheese
- 2 tomatoes

Preparation:

1. First you need to cook the pasta, since it will take time to rest. To mix the dough, you can use a bowl, but traditionally Italians do everything right on the table or on a large wooden cutting board - pour flour on the hill, in the middle make a groove like a volcano crater where eggs are broken, pour oil and add a pinch of salt. Then you need to start mixing the dough with the fork, adding a little flour to the liquid center, gradually the fork is put on hold, and the dough is already kneaded. The dough will be very tight, so it takes a little strength to get it mixed. Finished dough rolled into a bowl and put in a bowl, oiled, covered with a film and give a rest for 20-30 minutes.
2. While the dough is suitable, you can prepare a meat filling. In the cup Instant Pot pour a little oil and turn on the "Frying" mode. Onion, carrot and pepper chop and fry in oil. Add spices, salt and mince to them, continue to fry. After 20 minutes, when the stuffing is fried, add the tomato paste to it. If there is only one bowl for the Instant Pota, then the sauce should be transferred to another dish, and the bowl should be washed. If there are other bowls, the stuffing can simply be set aside.
3. At this stage, the dough is ready, it can be rolled to thin layers with your hands or with the help of a paste machine. You can make the sheets round the diameter of the bowl Instant Pot.

4. Next, you need to prepare all the other ingredients - rub the cheese and get out the refrigerator cream, so they are at room temperature.
5. We begin to collect the designer - on the bottom of the bowl, richly lubricated with butter, put the dough, top the meat sauce, sprinkle with cheese and pour a little cream. If a béchamel sauce is used, it should be poured directly onto the dough. So, you can continue until the dough or filling ends. The last layer of the dough should be covered with lasagna. From above it should be covered with mugs of fresh tomatoes and sprinkled with cheese.
6. Put a bowl of lasagna in the Instant Pota on a mode at which it will cook as you want. In the "Quenching" mode, it will be prepared more slowly, but it will be juicier. And on the "Baking" or "Porridge" cooking will go faster, but the lasagna will be drier and rosy.

Cabbage rolls in the Instant Pot

Ingredients:

- cabbage - 1 piece
- minced meat or chicken - 1/2 kg
- steamed rice - 1,5 cups
- onion - 2 pieces
- tomato paste - 2 tablespoons
- carrots - 1 piece
- sour cream or mayonnaise - 2 tablespoons
- vegetable oil
- salt, spices, pepper

Preparation:

1. Gently cut out of the head of a cob, so as not to damage cabbage leaves.
2. Pour in a large pot of water, boil it, we lower the cabbage leaves for a couple of minutes.
3. We clean onions and carrots from the peel. Onions should be finely chopped cubes, grate the carrots.
4. In the saucepan pour oil, put all the carrots and half of the chopped onions.
5. In the programs we find the "Frying" or "Baking" mode, we pass onions and carrots to the transparency of the onions.
6. Rinse the rice under running water.
7. We spread the vegetables from the Instant Pot in a bowl, put the rice there, the remaining onion and stuffing.
8. Add spices, salt, pepper, the whole stuffing for cabbage rolls is well mixed.
9. In the middle of each sheet, we put a spoonful of filling, wrap the edges of the cabbage leaf with an envelope so that the filling does not fall out during the preparation.
10. We again lubricate the cup of the Instant Pot oil, we put the stuffed cabbage into each other tightly.
11. Turn on the program "Baking", set the timer for 10 minutes.
12. After that, pour boiling water in the Instant Pot, water should not completely hide cabbage leaves, leave 1 cm.
13. We put the program "Quenching", the operating time of the Instant Pot is 40 minutes.
14. We prepare the sauce for cabbage rolls, for this mix the tomato paste with sour cream or mayonnaise, add a glass of water, a little salt.

15. When the regime time is over, pour the cabbage sauce over and continue cooking on the same regime for another 40 minutes.
16. We leave the cooked cabbage leaves in the Instant Pot for 10 minutes.

Potatoes with minced meat in an Instant Pot

Ingredients:
- Minced meat - 400g
- Potatoes - 9-10 pieces
- Bow
- Mayonnaise - 3 tablespoons
- Salt, pepper, spices

Preparation:
1. We peel potatoes, мея. Cut into cubes or circles. If the potatoes are young, then it can be cut into large slices, it is quickly brewed.
2. Onions finely chopped. If desired, you can again skip the minced meat through a meat grinder with onions, so it will become juicier.
3. Mix the stuffing, onions and potatoes. Add spices and mayonnaise. If you like a more piquant taste, you can put tomato paste and mustard. Also give variety to the dish mushrooms or bouillon cube.
4. Turn on the "Baking" mode, we set the time - 60 minutes.
5. When the signal for the end of cooking sounds, sprinkle the dish finely chopped, fresh greens.

Delicious cutlets in a multi-bar steamer in an Instant Pot

Ingredients:
- stuffing - 600 g
- bread crumbs - 2-3 tablespoons
- carrots - 1 piece
- onions - 1 piece
- garlic
- herbs - 2 tablespoons
- mayonnaise - 1 tablespoon
- salt pepper

Preparation:
1. Before the preparation begins, you need to prepare all the necessary equipment, namely you will need deep dishes, in which you should place minced meat.
2. After that it is necessary to drive in the egg, add salt and pepper, and not many breadcrumbs.
3. Also, for the taste, you can add shabby garlic and carrots to a fine grater. After that, you must mix everything thoroughly.
4. Further, in minced meat, it is necessary to assemble well-crushed herbs, dill or parsley, or both. Greenery will give steamed cutlets a strong, pleasant aroma.
5. The next stage of cooking is to achieve the most pleasant future taste of the dish and create a soft texture. This can be obtained if you add a tablespoon of mayonnaise to the stuffing.
6. And at the last stage it is already possible to proceed with the formation of small cutlets, which must be placed in the steamer cup. In the pot of the Instant Pot, you should pour three cups of water, then place the dishes with our cutlets in the Instant Pot and put in the "steaming" mode.
7. Preparation takes 30 minutes, after which cutlets can be obtained and served with any side dish, sauce or salad. The Instant Pot signal will let us know that the dish is cooked.

Couple cutlets in a Instant Pot

Ingredients:

- Beef and pork forcemeat - 700 g
- 1 potato
- 2 chicken eggs
- Onion - 2 pieces
- 1 piece of garlic
- Salt, black ground pepper
- 1 tablespoon of semolina

Preparation:

1. If you use ready-made stuffing, mix 3 to 2 beef and pork minced beans and mix this mass well. If you do not have ready, then you can cut pork and beef into small pieces and pass through a meat grinder.
2. Break two medium eggs into minced meat, season with salt and pepper.
3. Take garlic, brush and wash it, and then wipe it on a fine grater.
4. Then take one potato, also peel it and finely chop.
5. Peel the onion and twist it through the meat grinder.
6. Next, blend the grated onions, potatoes and garlic and add this mass to the stuffing.
7. Soak one tablespoon of semolina for ten minutes in water or milk, and then add it to the stuffing.
8. All the ingredients are mixed well with the minced meat so that a homogeneous mass is obtained.
9. Now form their resulting minced small-shaped cutlets. Beat them well between your hands.
10. Then go to the preparation of the Instant Pot. Pour water into the special bowl.
11. Take a special stand for steaming and install it.
12. Put the cutlets there.
13. Set the timer for forty minutes and turn on steam cooking.

Macaroni "in a Fleet" in a Instant Pot

Ingredients:

- minced meat - 300 g
- pasta - 1 pack
- carrots - 1 piece
- onion - 1 piece
- vegetable oil - 1 tablespoon
- water 1.5 liters
- salt, spices, herbs
- Bay leaf

Preparation:

1. Mine and we clean carrots, rub it on a small grater.
2. Peel the onion from the peel, cut into small pieces.
3. We pour water into the Instant Pot, select the "Pasta" program in the menu and set the timer for 15 minutes.
4. After the signal of readiness, add macaroni, vegetables, sunflower oil and minced meat to the water. If you do not have minced meat at home, but do not want to run to the store, but there is stew, then you can replace one another, such pasta also turns out delicious.
5. Pepper, salt, add spices and bay leaf. Stirring.
6. Press the "Start" command again, so that the immediate preparation of the dish begins.

Tasty meatballs in sour cream sauce in a Instant Pot

Ingredients:
- carrots - 1 piece
- sour cream - 4 tablespoons
- egg - 1 piece
- salt
- rice - 1 glass
- bulb -1 piece
- spice
- minced meat - 750 g
- water - 4 cups
- flour - 2 tablespoons
- tomato paste - 2 tablespoons

Preparation:
1. Mincemeat with salt, add rice, egg, sprinkle with pepper, stir, form meatballs.
2. Carrot cut into thin strips, peeled onions cut into cubes.
3. Prepare the fill: combine tomato with sour cream, add flour, water, salt and favorite spices, stir until homogeneous.
4. Put half the sliced vegetables in the bowl of the Instant Pot and lay the meatballs on them.
5. Top the other half of the vegetables, pour in the fill, then select the "Quenching" mode and set the timer for 1 hour.

Meatballs in the Instant Pot

Ingredients:

- Minced beef - 300 g
- Minced chicken - 200 g
- Garlic - 2 pieces
- Onion - 1 piece
- Tomato paste - 1-2 tablespoons
- Salt
- Pepper

Preparation:

1. Mix two types of minced meat - beef and chicken.
2. With the help of a cooking grater we grind a very finely peeled bulb.
3. Grind garlic on the same grater.
4. To the meat assortment add the onions, garlic and mix this mass carefully, add the spices to taste.
5. With wet hands we make meatballs, the shape of the meatballs to your taste, usually they are made in the form of small balls.
6. Put tomato paste in a separate bowl. Dense paste diluted with plain water to the state of liquid sour cream.
7. At the bottom of the Instant Pot capacity we put semi-finished products.
8. Fill meatballs with diluted tomato paste.
9. We cook meatballs in the Instant Pot in the "Quenching" mode for 1 hour.
10. The meatballs in the Instant Pot are ready.

Meat casserole with mashed potatoes

Ingredients:

- Minced pork meat - 400 g
- Potatoes - 8-9 pieces
- Bow green - 2 feathers
- Cheese hard - 150-200 g
- Vegetable oil - 1 tablespoon
- Salt

Preparation:

1. Potatoes without peel are boiled in salted water until cooked. From cold potatoes we make soft mashed potatoes.
2. In the minced meat, add salt to taste.
3. Hard cheese rubbed on a greater.
4. We cover the bottom of the multiquark cup with parchment paper and pour the vegetable oil, gently distributing it throughout the bottom. We spread half the potatoes on the butter, distribute it all over the bottom of the bowl.
5. Potatoes salt to taste. Sprinkle a small piece of cheese and chopped finely onions.
6. All the meat is evenly spread on cheese and onions.
7. Mincemeat is sprinkled with a piece of hard cheese.
8. On top, put some cheese, the remaining potatoes and cheese again. Sprinkle with spring onions. We cook the meat pie in the Instant Pot in the "Bake" mode for 1 hour.
9. Let the casserole with meat mince cool down and then extract it from the bowl of the Instant Pot.
10. The meat casserole in the Instant Pot is ready.

Buckwheat with minced meat

Ingredients:

- Minced beef - 350 g
- Buckwheat - 1 glass
- Carrots - 1 piece
- Onion - 1 piece
- Tomato - 1 piece
- Butter - 30 g
- Black pepper powder
- Salt
- Water - 2 cups

Preparation:

1. Carrot cut into strips.
2. Finely chop onion.
3. Blanch tomato, peel and finely chop.
4. Put the butter in the bowl of the Instant Pot, add chopped onions, carrots, tomatoes and fry in the "Frying" mode.
5. After 5 minutes, add minced meat, salt, pepper.
6. Stir and fry minced meat with vegetables in the same mode for another 15 minutes.
7. Add the buckwheat, salt, pepper to the bowl of the Instant Pota.
8. Pour in water and mix.
9. Cooking buckwheat with meat in an Instant Pot, setting the "Pilaf".

Khanum with meat and potatoes

Ingredients:
- Wheat Flour - 600 g
- Water - 1 glass
- Salt - 1 teaspoon
- Egg of chicken - 1 piece
- Vegetable oil - 2 tablespoons
- Minced meat - 900 g
- Onion - 400 g
- Potatoes raw - 2-3 pieces
- Salt
- Black pepper powder

Preparation:
1. We prepare the dough for khanum. Sift the flour into a bowl.
2. Separately mix water, salt, egg and vegetable oil. We connect water with flour.
3. We knead the elastic dough.
4. We wrap the dough in a plastic bag and put it in the refrigerator.
5. We will do the preparation of the filling. Onion cut into small cubes or semirings. Add salt, pepper and grate your hands to make the onion softer.
6. Add minced meat to the onion. If necessary, salt again. Mix well with your hands.
7. Raw potatoes are finely chopped or shredded on a greater for a Korean carrot and mixed in minced meat. If the stuffing is not very fat, you can add chilled butter, grated.
8. We prepare the khanum. The dough is divided into 3 equal parts and rolled into a layer not more than 1 mm thick.
9. The surface of the dough should be greased with vegetable oil, so the layers of the roll do not stick together.
10. Uniform layer distributes the filling on the surface of the dough and fold it into a roll.
11. We cut the edges of the roll. Thus, we form two more rolls.
12. The bottom of the sieve and the surface of the roll are greased with vegetable oil. Thus, the roll does not stick to the sieve and will have a brilliant appearance when finished.
13. We shift the khanum into a sieve of steamers or Instant Pot.

14. We put the khanum to prepare for a couple. The cooking time is 40-60 minutes.
15. This dish is usually served with two sauces: tomato onion and sour cream.

Spaghetti bolognese

Ingredients:
- Spaghetti - 400 g
- Cheese hard - 100 g
- Minced beef - 300 g
- Tomatoes - 2 pieces
- Tomato paste - 2 tablespoons
- Onion - 600 g
- Garlic - 3 pieces
- Vegetable oil - 4 tablespoons
- Salt
- Black pepper powder
- Greenery
- Water - 2 l

Preparation:
1. In a bowl Instant Pot pour 1 liter of water, bring to a boil in the "Soup". Salt and pepper the boiling water, put spaghetti and cook for 10 minutes in "Pasta" mode.
2. Finished spaghetti rinse.
3. Finely chop the onions.
4. Grate the cheese on a fine grater.
5. Finely chop the peeled tomatoes.
6. To prepare the Bolognese sauce, pour the vegetable oil on the bottom of the Instant Pot bowl, put the finely chopped onions and put garlic through the press, mix. Choose the program "Baking", cooking time - 40 minutes.
7. After 3 minutes add the finely chopped tomatoes. Add the tomato paste and continue cooking for another 5 minutes.
8. Put in the bowl Instant Pot forcemeat, salt, pepper, stir, close the lid and simmer for 10 minutes.
9. Add 1 liter of water, stir, close the lid and cook the Bolognese meat sauce until the end time.
10. When serving spaghetti sprinkle with grated cheese, pour on the meat sauce of the Bolognese and decorate with greens.

Casserole with minced meat and vegetables

Ingredients:

- Minced meat - 600 g
- Zucchini - 1 piece
- Potatoes - 3 pieces
- Tomatoes - 2 pieces
- Bulgarian pepper - 1 piece
- Onion - 1 piece
- Onion green - 10 g
- Egg - 1 piece
- Milk - 50 ml
- Vegetable oil - 2 tablespoons
- Sour Cream - 2 tablespoons
- Salt - 1 teaspoon
- Black pepper
- Mushrooms fried

Preparation:

1. Peel and finely chop zucchini.
2. Cut the onion.
3. Mix the onions and zucchini in the bowl of the Instant Pot.
4. Turn on the Instant Pot in the "Frying" mode for 30 minutes and fry the vegetables for 10 minutes.
5. Cut the smaller tomatoes.
6. After the onions and zucchini are slightly fried, add the tomatoes to them and fry for 15 minutes, but do not overcook.
7. At this time, cut the Bulgarian pepper in half rings.
8. Cut potatoes into semicircular plates.
9. Chop finely green onions.
10. And mix the greens with potatoes.
11. Beat with egg or egg whisk with milk, salt and pepper.
12. Half of the egg-milk mixture is poured into the potatoes, and half poured into minced meat.
13. Add fried vegetables and stir well.
14. In the Instant Pot lay the sleeve for baking - so it is easier to remove the casserole from the bowl without destroying it.
15. Stack vegetables in layers: first potatoes and Bulgarian pepper.

16. Then a layer of stuffing.
17. And again, the potatoes.
18. To prepare a casserole with minced meat in an Instant Pot in the mode "Baking" exactly 65 minutes, no less.
19. After that, slightly cool the casserole, and then take it out with the sleeve. Carefully remove the sleeve.
20. Pour the casserole over with sour cream.

Meat pie with meat

Ingredients:

- Kefir - 1/2 cup
- Flour - 2/3 cup
- Egg - 2 pieces
- Mayonnaise - 120 g
- Soda - 1/2 teaspoon
- Salt - 1/3 teaspoon
- Pork - 300 g
- Onion - 1 piece
- Tomato paste - 2 tablespoons
- Salt
- Spice

Preparation:

1. Cut the pork into pieces.
2. Place the meat in the blender bowl.
3. Grind the pork until smooth.
4. Ingredients for the filling are ready.
5. Onions, peeled from the top layer, cut into cubes.
6. Heat the frying pan, add the vegetable oil and fry the onions.
7. Then add a pork mince in a frying pan with onions, fry for a few minutes.
8. Add the tomato paste, add salt, add spices and simmer for another 5 minutes. The filling for the jellied pie is ready.
9. How to prepare a dough for a jellied pie:
10. Prepare all the necessary ingredients for the test. It should be noted that about 4 servings are obtained from this amount of ingredients. Pie in diameter of 15 sm. If the form for baking is much more, increase quantity of ingredients in 2 times.
11. Add half a teaspoon of soda to the sour milk product. Leave for 5-10 minutes.
12. After a time, the volume of yogurt increases by 2 times.
13. Beat the eggs and salt.
14. Add the mayonnaise and mix.
15. Gradually stir in the flour. Mix the dough thoroughly with a mixer. The dough turns liquid.

16. Lubricate the bottom of the bowl with vegetable oil, sprinkle with breadcrumbs. You can use parchment paper to make it easier to extract the finished pie.
17. Pour half the dough into the bowl.
18. Put the stuffing.
19. Pour our cake with the second half of the batter.
20. Enable multicasting, set the "Baking" mode for 40 minutes. This time will be enough to bake a cake. But it all depends on its size.
21. When the cake is ready, let it cool down. Then remove from the bowl.

Potato casserole with meat balls

Ingredients:

- Minced meat 500 g
- Potatoes - 800-1000 g
- Carrots - 1 piece
- Onion - 1 piece
- Garlic - 1 piece
- Eggs - 2 pieces
- Manka - 3 tablespoons
- Mayonnaise - 5 tablespoons
- Nutmeg - 1/3 teaspoon
- Salt
- Pepper
- Fresh dill
- Vegetable oil

Preparation:

1. Rub carrots on a large grater and cut the onions into cubes. Heat the frying pan, pour in the sunflower oil, fry the onions and carrots until lightly browned.
2. Scrub the potatoes on a large grater, add the mango, eggs, fried onions with carrots and mayonnaise. To make the potatoes not dark, you can add the juice of onions, then the potatoes will remain light.
3. Add the spices. Mix everything thoroughly.
4. In the baking dish, add sunflower oil, grease all the walls and the bottom. Lay out the base of the casserole.
5. With moistened hands, form a meatball with minced meat. Mince for this salt and pepper. In the basis of the casserole put the meatballs, slightly pressing them into the potatoes.
6. You can prepare a potato pudding in an Instant Pot or send it to a preheated oven for 180 minutes for 40 minutes.
7. Potato casserole with meat balls is ready.

Lazy dumplings

Ingredients:

- Flour - 500 g
- Egg - 1 piece
- Water - 200 ml
- Salt - 0.5 teaspoon
- Minced meat - 500 g
- Onion - 2 pieces
- Carrots - 1 piece
- Champignons - 300 g
- Salt
- Black pepper powder
- Vegetable oil - 20 ml
- Garlic - 3 pieces
- Water - 200 ml
- Sour cream 150 g
- Greenery - 4 g

Preparation:

1. For the dough, stir the egg in water, add salt and sprinkle with flour. Knead the dough as if it were ordinary dumplings. Let the dough rest for 30 minutes, wrapping it in a film.
2. Prepare the filling. Cut onion finely and add 2/3 of ground meat, salt and pepper.
3. Mix well.
4. Rub carrots on a large grater.
5. Cut champignons into plates.
6. Turn the Instant Pot into the "Frying" mode for 10 minutes, pour the oil into the bowl, fry the carrots, the rest of the onions and champignons, add the garlic through the press, add to the frying.
7. Roll out the dough thinly.
8. Put on the dough forcemeat, level.
9. Roll the dough with stuffing into a roll.
10. Cut the roll into pieces, 3 cm thick.
11. Put the dumplings on the fried vegetables and add water.
12. Turn the Instant Pot into the "Baking" mode, cook lazy dumplings in the Instant Pot 30 minutes.

13. For the sauce cut the greens and mix it with sour cream.
14. At the end of the program, dumplings put on a dish, pour broth with fried.
15. Serve lazy dumplings with sour cream.

Meatballs in tomato sauce

Ingredients:

- Minced pork meat - 500 g
- Onion - 2 pieces
- Carrots - 1 piece
- Rice - 0,75 cups
- Mayonnaise - 0,5 cups
- Tomato paste - 140 g
- Eggs - 2 pieces
- Bay leaf - 2 pieces
- Water - 1 l
- Vegetable oil
- Salt
- Black pepper powder

Preparation:

1. In the mince pour rice and drive 2 eggs.
2. To stir thoroughly.
3. Peel onion and finely chop.
4. In the mince add 1 onion, mayonnaise, salt and pepper to taste.
5. Stir the mince thoroughly.
6. In a frying pan in vegetable oil fry the meatballs. To form them is most comfortable with hands dipped in cold water. I advise making meatballs small, as they will increase.
7. Fry for 4-5 minutes on each side.
8. Thus, fry all the meatballs, put them in a bowl Instant Pot, greased with vegetable oil.
9. Carrot clean and grate on a fine grater.
10. In a heated frying pan with vegetable oil, fry 1 onion until golden.
11. Add the carrots, stir. Fry until soft carrots, for 5-7 minutes.
12. Put the fried onion and carrots on the meatballs and rice and pour the tomato paste.
13. Pour water, add bay leaf. Salt and pepper. Do not mix.
14. Stew meatballs in tomato sauce on the "Quenching" mode for 1 hour.

Printed in Great Britain
by Amazon